First published in 2012 by Awa Press, Level Three,
11 Vivian Street, Wellington 6011, New Zealand.

ISBN 978-1-877551-61-1

Designed and typeset by Donna Cross, threeeyes.co.nz
Printed by Everbest Printing Co. Ltd, China

Find more great books at awapress.com.

Vinacular

A WINE LOVER'S A-Z

SCOTT KENNEDY · JOHN SAKER

AWA PRESS

VINTRO

There are many worlds within our world. You know you're in a new one when you have trouble understanding what is being said around you. Jargon, patois, *vern*acular – whatever name you give them, these other tongues are essential keys to understanding the workings of their respective worlds. By their lingo shall you know them.

Language, in this sense, is like art – it represents a different way of looking at life. So when Scott Kennedy – whose wonderful art adorns our walls at home – came to me with the germ of an idea for this book, that connection and its possibilities were immediately appealing. I'd be the straight man and offer an explanation of a colourful wine term I had selected. Scott, with his kind eye and mad sense of humour, would then take the concept somewhere else entirely.

Vinacular does not set out to provide a comprehensive decoding of the argot of vino. Think of it more as a rollicking, selective dash through the wine world. You may well learn something, but the authors' larger wish is that, as with a glass of wine, by the end of it you're a little happier than you were at the beginning.

JOHN SAKER

Angel's Share

Every year without fail it happens; angels come down
and slip unseen into cellars. There they make merry
by taking to the wine resting
in barrel. (Less poetic
souls might call it
evaporation.)

BEAD

Ascending lines of bubbles enliven every glass of

champagne, each like a fine pearl necklace.

Real pearls?

Someone thought not…

because we call the bubbles "the bead".

B

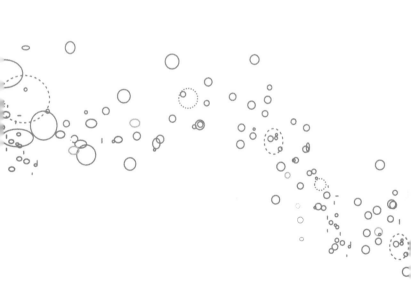

Closed

When a wine is "closed" it is showing its youth
– its smells and tastes come over all shy and quiet.
It can be weeks, months, or even years before
it opens up shop.

Dionysus

Sometimes shown with the horns of a bull,
wine's own god lived life on the wild side,
a symbol of unreasoned behaviour and
spontaneity. The original party animal.

E NTRY-LEVEL W INES

Entry-level wines are like ground-floor apartments.

It's where you start out, pay less, get no kind of

a view and wonder how good it must be

up there in the penthouse.

(Or how hideous down in the basement.)

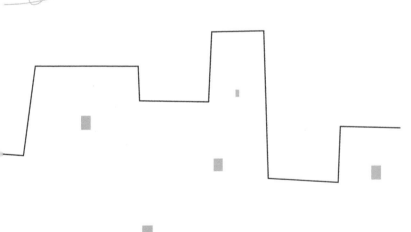

F

FIASCO

At one time, the fiasco *was* Italian Chianti. But those funky bottles with the round bottoms all covered in straw are becoming too expensive to make. A fiasco-free Italy? How's that going to work?

GLOBALISATION

Globalisation has given us a
wine world that has grown and shrunk
at the same time. There's more wine
than ever, but less diversity.
And we were told it was
all about choice...

HERBACEOUS

When you taste herbaceous
flavours, you're tasting a
colour – green. It's not
easy being green if you're
a red wine; whites like
sauvignon blanc and
semillon are another story.

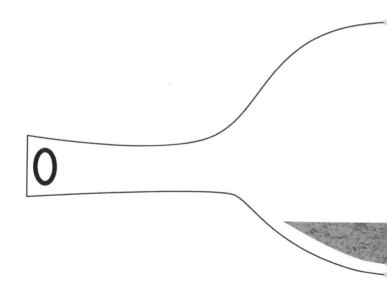

INVESTMENT

Investment
opportunity: buy a
case of fine wine
from a great vintage,
store it in a cool dark place,
and with every passing
year its value will rise.
Like any investment
it's not without risks, the
big one being your
desire to "see how it's
coming along".

J

JAMMY

When grapes see too much sun and heat,
the wine is dark, soft and syrupy-sweet.
When the producer sells it, you could call
it money for jam.

KERO

Despite its smell you don't drill for it,

nor can your car run on it.

Older riesling develops that kerosene-like flavour

which the French call "goût de pétrole".

All it fuels is a desire to maybe have another.

LENGTH

Like a man
who can't stop
telling you
something,
a mouthful
of wine can go
on and on...
but in the most
enjoyable way.
You long for
wines with
length.

L

Minerality

Wine rocks, but does it really taste that way? "Minerality" is one of those tasting terms that means different things to different people (and is not a word you'll find in the dictionary). Flavours akin to chalk, earth and iron, as well as textural hardness, often trigger the "M" word.

M

NOBLE ROT

When noble rot, aka *Botrytis cinerea*,
takes hold of a bunch of grapes they look
ugly and decrepit, ignoble even.
Don't be fooled, because on the inside life is sweet.
Wine of honeyed beauty, like an uninhibited
butterfly, is waiting to escape.

Oaky

Many a mighty oak tree has gone from housing
squirrels to housing wine. Spending time in an oak
barrel alters a wine's taste and structure. But if
a winemaker is wooed to distraction by wood, the
taste of timber takes over. We call those wines "oaky".

O

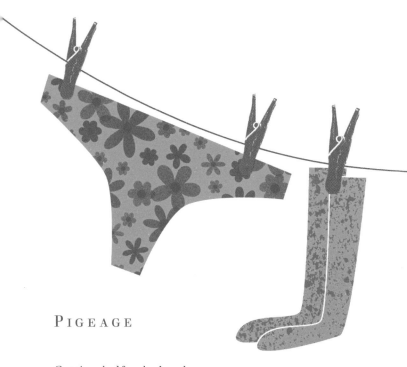

PIGEAGE

Getting half-naked and
sloshing around in a vat of fermenting wine... the
ancient French practice of *pigeage* helps the juice gain
more colour and tannin from the grapeskins. There's
no feeling quite like it – although your undies
will never be the same again.

P

Quaffer

Quaff a quaffer to quickly quench,
but factor in the quality quotient,
for down so easy can go quite queasy.
"He made me a quaffer I should have refused!"

ROUND

Lying idle in a cellar, a wine
doesn't get fat, just more shapely.
It drops those hard edges and
becomes "round". You'll find
these corners a pleasure
to negotiate.

R

SMELL

Smell – that primitive,
animal sense – is also
that unappreciated,
neglected sense.
We've stopped thinking
about what our noses
bring us. Not around
wine though. It's OK
to poke your schnozz
right into a glass and
concentrate on all the
things you smell there.
Sniff away, you beast.

S

T

TEARS

Swirl a glass of wine and watch its inner walls weep.
It's not upset because it's about to vanish forever down
your throat. The cause of those tears is that old
trigger of emotion – the presence of alcohol.

Unctuous

An unctuous person so wants to
be your best friend. An unctuous
wine is similar – velvety,
often sweet, rich, intense,
i.e. trying far too hard.

VOLATILE

There's nothing risqué
about a wine that is
volatile. It will smell
like vinegar – or
worse, like nail polish
remover. This occurs
when one or more of
the volatile acids that
inhabit wine bolt out
the door and can't
be reined in. Best not
to put such a wine in
your mouth, or
you'll start feeling
volatile too.

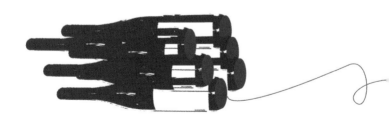

V

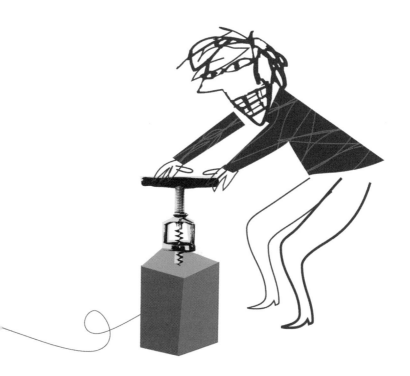

WINEMAKER

"I'm a winemaker," said the man.

"And me?" piped up the vine. "I work with earth and sunlight to make ripe fruit, without which you'd have nothing. Am I not a winemaker, too?"

W

X FACTOR

Wines that leave you with a palate memory nothing
can wash away; wines you want to talk about, but then
you find yourself saying something like "Xxxx!"
These are wines with an X factor.

Young

When wines are young they're bright and
bouncy, but also often ungainly and awkward.
Some settle down and become more interesting
with age; others just never grow up.

Y

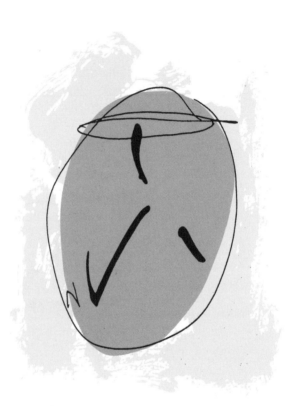

Z

Zzzzzzz

Feeling drowsy?
It must be
that glass of
wine you've been
enjoying as you've
turned the pages
of this book.
It can have that
effect.
Sleep well.

SCOTT KENNEDY

Scott Kennedy is a New Zealand-based illustrator whose work appears in books, magazines and newspapers in New Zealand, Australia, Canada and the United States. His captivating paintings and prints are held in galleries and private collections around the world. He creates the award-winning covers for Awa Press's *Ginger* series.

JOHN SAKER

John Saker writes about wine for New Zealand's *Cuisine* and *Sunday* magazines. He is the author of two previous wine books: *Pinot Noir: The New Zealand Story* and Awa Press's perennially popular *How to Drink a Glass of Wine*. John's interest in wine began when he played professional basketball in France. The sport also inspired his acclaimed essay *Tracing the Arc* in the *Four Winds* series.